Excel
Basic Skills

Year 3
Ages 8–9

Handwriting

Get the Results You Want!

Ada Munro & Ivy Morgan

PASCAL
PRESS

ISBN 978 1 74125 736 6

Pascal Press Pty Ltd
PO Box 250
Glebe NSW 2037
(02) 9198 1748
www.pascalpress.com.au

Publisher: Vivienne Joannou
Edited by Rosemary Peers
Cover and page design by Sonia Woo
Typeset by lj Design (Julianne Billington)
Printed by Vivar Printing/Green Giant Press

Contents

Progress tracker

Colour the signpost when you complete each challenge.

Revise Foundation printing on pages 11–17.

Make drop-in joins on pages 28–30.

Make horizontal joins on pages 31–38.

Revise cursive writing on pages 80–87.

Add exits on pages 18–19.

Add entries on pages 20–21.

Make diagonal joins on pages 22–27.

Know letters that don't join—see pages 39–40.

Practise whole words in cursive on pages 41–72.

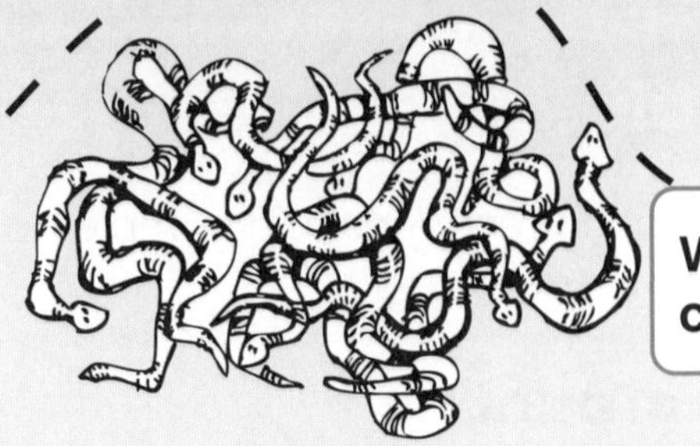

Write sentences in cursive on pages 73–79.

Try some extra advanced joins on pages 88–91.

Assess my own handwriting on pages 92–93.

Introduction

Welcome to the wonderful world of NSW Foundation Style Cursive handwriting.

The activities in this book will help your child:

- learn how to join letters in cursive handwriting
- develop neat, legible and fluent cursive handwriting
- learn to value neat and fluent cursive handwriting as a fast and effective method of communication
- expand and enrich their vocabulary
- develop their knowledge about words and their understanding about how language works
- develop their ability to build word families using prefixes and suffixes
- develop their phonic knowledge—the sounds in words and the letters that spell those sounds
- improve their fine motor control, visual discrimination and coordination.

Handwriting helps children's spelling in two main ways. First, the movement used to write a word, and therefore the letter sequences involved in writing it, become automatic. Some people write a word in the air when trying to spell it out loud because they are relying on muscle memory and the feel of writing the word to remember how to spell it.

Second, when you write a word you look at it and focus on the sequence of letters. Writing words neatly imprints on the brain the way they look when spelt correctly. Children's literacy development is supported by a neat, legible handwriting style with letters of consistent shape and size. Research has proven that children with good control of handwriting usually do better in spelling and reading in the early years. As in all things, practice makes perfect!

The handwriting practice activities in this book use challenging words to expand children's vocabulary and spelling knowledge.

An overview of NSW Foundation Style Cursive is included on pages 94–95.

How to use this book

Children need to begin at the front of the book and work through the pages in sequence. Working through the pages out of sequence is not recommended because the letter joins are presented and then practised and revised in an appropriate learning sequence.

Progress tracker

The progress tracker on pages 4 and 5 is a quick reference that you can use to check your child's progress through the skills and activities in the book. Your child can colour each label that corresponds to a completed skill or activity page.

Revision of printing

The book begins with a revision of the movements required to form the printed letters of the NSW Foundation Style and to remind children where letters start and finish. Downward diagonal stroke and zigzag letters are dealt with first, then clockwise letters and anticlockwise letters. It is important that children understand where letters begin and end because this is how letters are joined in cursive handwriting. Upper-case letters, numerals and punctuation markers are also revised in the early pages.

Exits and entries

The next section of the book focuses children's attention on letters that have exit flicks or entries. Exit flicks are used to join the letter to the following letter in a word.

A student tip is provided at the top of each page with sample letters to show how the letter is formed and how it sits within the writing guidelines.

Some letters have an exit on the main line (*a*, *d*, *h*, *i*, *k*, *l*, *m*, *n*, *t*, *u*). Some letters have their exit on the top solid line (*v*, *w*) or at a letter's tail (*q*). Some letters don't have exits because they end facing backwards. They are the anticlockwise letters *b*, *g*, *j*, *p*, *s*, *y*. Note that in Year 3 NSW Foundation Style Cursive handwriting these letters do not join to the letters that come after them. Entries on letters *i*, *j*, *p*, *r*, *u*, *v*, *w*, *m* and *n* are used to join the letter to the letter that comes before it in a word.

Introducing the joins

This section of the book deals with the three ways to join letters: diagonal joins, drop-in joins and horizontal joins. It also covers letters which don't join at this stage of learning cursive.

The joins are taught and practised using pairs of letters before students are given any words to write.

These pages each include a Student tip with a diagram and an instructional text that describes how the join works.

Practising joins in words

The practice section of the book includes dozens of words to trace and copy.

These words have been chosen because they include the **specific joins** that your child will practise but also because they will **enrich your child's language**. They provide **spelling challenges** as well as opportunities to focus your child's attention on prefixes, suffixes (including plurals), word families, compound words and other aspects of language.

Help your child use the words in conversations and in their writing.

At the bottom of each page is a parent tip. As well as handwriting reminders, the tips include spelling or vocabulary teaching points and other information for parents.

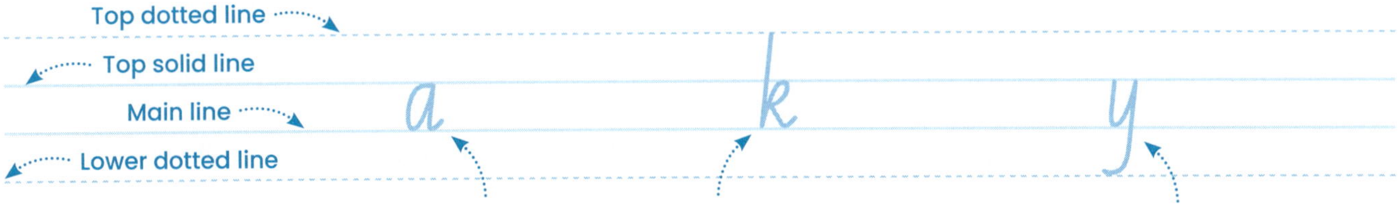

short letter
This lower-case letter sits between the top solid line and main line.

tall letter
The body of *k* sits between the top solid line and main line. It's a tall letter so its downstroke starts at the top dotted line.

long letter
Lower-case *y* is a long letter. Its body fits between the top solid line and main line. Its tail reaches the lower dotted line.

The right-hand page of every double-page spread includes a **student tip**. Most of these have diagrams that remind children about aspects of the particular focus join.

Writing cursive sentences

There are seven pages with alliterative sentences for students to trace and copy. The sentences include words used on the vocabulary pages in order to reinforce the meanings and spellings of the words and to ensure that every join is consolidated. The sentences are lighthearted. Encourage your child to use words on the vocabulary pages to create their own alliterative sentences.

Revision

Revision pages include rhyme challenges, word-family challenges and writing labels.

The **rhyme challenges** present new words not used in the book so far. Children need to think of a rhyming word for each one. If they cannot think of one, they can look back through the vocabulary pages to find a word.

The **word-family challenges** present new words not used in the book so far. Children need to write two words belonging to the same family. Children can write verbs in different tenses (*ran, running*), adjectives (*runny*) and nouns (*runner*). Check your child's spelling.

The **labelling** activities provide opportunities for your child to practise their writing skills without the support of guidelines.

Extra advanced joins to try

These pages teach children how to join to *s* horizontally and diagonally, and how to join to *e* horizontally. These joins are mostly taught in Year 4. We are presenting them here for children to try. Do not be concerned if your child cannot manage these joins neatly at this stage.

Self-assessment

The self-assessment pages challenge children with printing and cursive speed tasks. The aim of self-assessment is for children to be critically reflective of their own work. As children mature they need to rely less on extrinsic reward or motivation and more on intrinsic motivation so they can strive for excellence and be pleased within themselves for a job they think they have done well. Encourage your child to be honest with themselves in their assessments and judge their efforts truthfully.

Tips for effective handwriting

- The poster on page 96 can be used by your child as a reminder of the three Ps of posture, pencil/pen grip and paper/page tilt. It can also help them develop self-correcting skills.

Tips for left-handed writers

- Ten per cent of people are left-handed and more boys than girls are left-handed. Being left-handed does not mean your child will have messy handwriting. It just means they will have a few extra challenges to overcome because the world is largely set up for right-handed people. In this book, students copy letter pairs or words underneath the sample provided. This ensures that left-handed children have a clear view of what they are copying.

- Left-handed writers have to *push* their pencil or pen rather than *pull* it, so writing is more difficult. Pulling is smoother and easier than pushing. Pushing means you are more likely to tear the paper or smudge the writing.
- Have your child hold their pencil or pen 2–3 cm from the tip. This is close enough to the tip to give them good control of the pencil but far enough away from the tip that they can see their writing.
- Make sure the shaft of the pencil or pen rests in the web of the hand between the thumb and forefinger.

Grip

- The grip should be relaxed and not hooked or cramped. Make sure your child keeps their wrist straight. This will avoid cramping but also allow your child to see their writing. They need to keep their hand below the writing line.
- Practising on a vertical chalkboard or whiteboard can help free up arm movements.

Sitting on the left

- In any situation where two children are sharing a desk or table for writing, the left-handed child should sit on the left side of the right-handed child so they don't bump arms when writing. Make sure there's space on the left to support the child's left arm.

Paper

- Tilt the page's left corner up and right side down for a left-handed student so the left-handed child can see the tip of the pencil and where they are writing. Tell them to use their right hand to hold the page steady. Use a start dot on the left side of the page to remind your child where to start.

> **TIP** Check that your child's classroom allows for a left-handed computer mouse and left-handed scissors.

Handwriting troubleshooting

- Efficient, fluent and legible handwriting is important for writing. When handwriting is slow and laboured, and when children have trouble reading their own handwriting, it leads to frustration and embarrassment at school. Children then avoid handwriting and it becomes a vicious cycle. Without practice they can't improve. Achieving success from the very beginning is important in supporting children's confidence as writers. Fast handwriting helps students get their thoughts onto paper quickly so their creativity can flow. Most children can improve their handwriting with practice and targeted intervention but some may always struggle.
- Parents can help identify issues early on before children's self-esteem is impacted, and to prevent the impact that poor handwriting has on other areas of learning, especially reading and spelling.

Watch your child in action as they write.

- How do they look? Comfortable or uncomfortable? Relaxed or tense?
- What are their wrists, arms, shoulders, fingers, etc. doing as they write?

Look at the writing your child is producing.

- Are the letters cramped, of irregular sizes or illegible?

Talk to your child about handwriting.

- Ask them how they feel about writing. Do they enjoy it/ avoid it? Do they value handwriting as a skill? If they find writing difficult, does it bother them? Are they worried about their handwriting? Do they care about handwriting? Have they seen you write (notes, messages, lists) to understand the importance of legible handwriting?

Handwriting problems can occur in these main areas:

Issue	What's needed	How to help
Speed and fluency	Fluency is needed. If your child is too slow, it indicates that they cannot write in cursive automatically (without thinking).	Your child needs to develop automaticity (where the joins and the letter sequences for spelling become automatic).
Joins and legibility	Muscle memory and automaticity	Have your child practise the joins in pairs of letters and in words. Describe the joins as your child writes, to draw on auditory memory as well as visual and motor memory.
Letters not sitting correctly on lines	Knowledge about where letters' entries and exits sit in relation to the guidelines; for example, *f* with a new tail and *q* with a long join	Revision and practice
Slope	Understanding that a consistent slope is required so that letters do not lean into each other or look cramped	Check the paper/page tilt. Help your child find an even and consistent slope that is comfortable for them.
Uneven and/or inconsistent space between letters and between words	Understanding how letters are joined, especially to anticlockwise letters and drop-in joins	Have your child practise writing and then reading what is written.
Pencil/Pen grip and pressure	Correct grip is essential for relaxed and fluid writing (see page 96) and to avoid wrist and finger strain.	Make sure pencil/pen and paper or other writing surface is appropriate for your child's stage of development.
Posture or body position	Correct body position and paper position to avoid wrist, arm, neck or shoulder strain	Check that your child is sitting correctly (see the poster on page 96). Do warm-ups and stretching.
Inconsistent formation of letters	Consistent letter formation for a positive impact on spelling. When letters in words look different each time a child writes them, it's hard for the child to develop any visual memory for the way the words should look or to develop any muscle memory for how it feels to write the word. This can affect your child's spelling.	Practice

Revision: printing line and zigzag letters

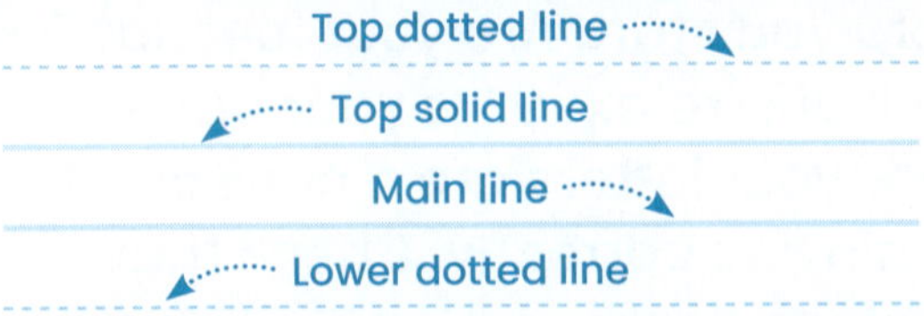

Remember to use the guidelines so that letters start and end in the correct places and letters are of a consistent size.

Trace then copy.

l t i x z f j l t i x z

f j l t i x z j l t i x

z j l t i x z j l t i x

Make words using only line and zigzag letters.

Revision: printing clockwise letters

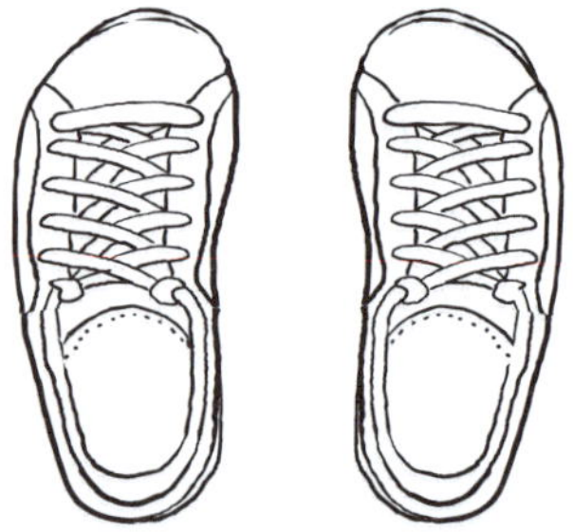

Check your posture before you start. Are your feet flat on the floor? Is your pencil grip relaxed? Is your page tilted correctly? Make sure your letters are a consistent size and sitting on the main line correctly. Check that your letters have a consistent slope.

Trace then copy.

m n r h b p k m n r h b

p k m n r h b p k m n r

h b p k m n r h b p k m

Make words using only clockwise letters and the letter *i*.

Revision: printing anticlockwise letters

Remember to make sure the space between letters in words and between words is even. Check that your printing is neat and that others find it easy to read.

Trace then copy.

u v w y a c o g q d e s

y a c o g q d e s u v w

d e s u v w y a c o g q

Make words using only anticlockwise letters.

Revision: printing upper-case letters

Write a proper noun for each letter.

		A	B
C	D	E	F
G	H	I	J
K	L	M	N
O	P	Q	R
S	T	U	V
W	X	Y	Z

Revision: printing upper-case letters

Complete the crossword using UPPER-CASE letters.

Down

1. black-and-white stripes
3. fierce fish
4. square poo
5. eucalyptus leaves
7. wildcat

Across

2. pollen power
5. leaping legs
6. tiny strength

kangaroo tiger zebra
shark ant koala wombat
bee

Revision: printing

A pangram is a sentence that contains every letter of the alphabet.

a b c d e f g h i j k l m n
o p q r s t u v w x y z

Trace and copy the pangrams.

The quick brown fox jumps
over the lazy dog.

We saw five boxing zombies
quickly run to jump the ditch.

Try to use every letter of the alphabet to write your own pangram.

Revision: numerals and punctuation

Trace then copy.

0 1 2 3 4 5 6 7 8 9

. . , , ? ? ! ! “ ” ‘ ’ : : ; ; – –

‘Why do we use punctuation

marks?’ asked Freya.

‘They make our meaning

clearer,’ replied Juan.

PARENT TIP: Discuss the names of the punctuation marks and how they are used to punctuate writing.

Adding exits

Exit flicks help move your pencil to the next letter to join it in cursive writing. Some exit flicks are at the main line: a d h i k l m n t u.

a h k

Track

a a a d d d h h h

i i i k k k l l l

Trace then copy.

a a a a d d d d h h h h

i i i i k k k k l l l l

a a a a d d d d h h h h

i i i i k k k k l l l l

Some exit flicks are at the top solid line: *v* and *w*. They have a little DIP at the top exit.

v w

Track

m m m n n n t t t

u u u v v v w w w

Trace then copy.

m m m m n n n n t t t t

u u u u v v v v w w w w

m m m m n n n n t t t t

u u u u v v v v w w w w

Adding entries

Some letters have entries. This is how these letters join from the previous letter: *i j m n p r u v w y*. You don't need to do entry flicks at the beginning of words.

i r p

Track

i i i j j j p p p
r r r y y y i j y

Trace then copy.

i i i i j j j j p p p p

r r r r y y y y i i i i

j j j j p p p p r r r r

y y y y i i i i j j j j

Some letters have exits as well as entries: *i m n u v w*. Notice that the entries are all at the top of the letters.

u w m

Track

u u u v v v w w w

m m m n n n u w m

Trace then copy.

u u u u v v v v w w w w

m m m m n n n n u u u u

v v v v w w w w m m m m

n n n n u u u u v v v v

Diagonal joins from short letters to short letters

A diagonal join goes from a letter's exit flick up to the next letter. The letters c and e have their own built-in exit flick. So go from there up to the next letter.

em ur ci nn

Trace

em ur ci
nn ax ex

Trace then copy.

ai am an ar au ax ci cr

cu ce ei ee em en er ex

eu ev ew ex im in ir mi

mn ni nn nu ue ui im

Trace then copy.

um ur ae ie me ne im

cu ce ei ee em en er

ai am an ar au ci cr

cu ce ei ee em en er

eu ev ew im in ir mi

mn ni nn nu ue ui im

Diagonal joins from short letters to long letters

A diagonal join takes your pencil from a letter's exit flick up to join to the next letter's entry.

ey up my

Trace

ey up my ey up

Trace then copy.

aj ap cy ey ep ej up

uy mp my ny aj ap cy

ey ep ej up uy mp my

my ny aj ap cy ey ep

Diagonal joins from tall letters

A diagonal join takes your pencil from a letter's exit flick up to join to the next letter's entry.

de kr tu

Trace

de tu he li kr

Trace then copy.

de di dr du he hi hu

ke ki kn kr ku le li

lm lu te ti tr tu de

di dr du he hi hu ke

Diagonal joins to tall letters

To join diagonally to a tall letter you need to go up and then carefully retrace down.

ch th tt

Trace

ch th tt ek ub

Trace then copy.

lt lk lb th tt kl ch

ah il ul ik ih nk nt

at ut ak el eh et dl

ab eb ib ub ck ct cl

Diagonal joins from q and z

The exit flick from the tail of the q has to go all the way up to meet the entry for the u. The bottom of the z is a wavy line that extends up to meet the next letter.

qu ze

Trace

qu ze za zi zl

Trace then copy.

z z z z z z z

qu za ze zi zo zu zl

qu za ze zi zo zu zl

qu za ze zi zo zu zl

Drop-in joins

The letters a c d g o q don't have entries to join them to letters that come before them. They drop into place onto the exit of the previous letter. Make that letter's exit flick longer than usual if you have to join it to a, c, d, g, o or q. Keep your letters evenly spaced.

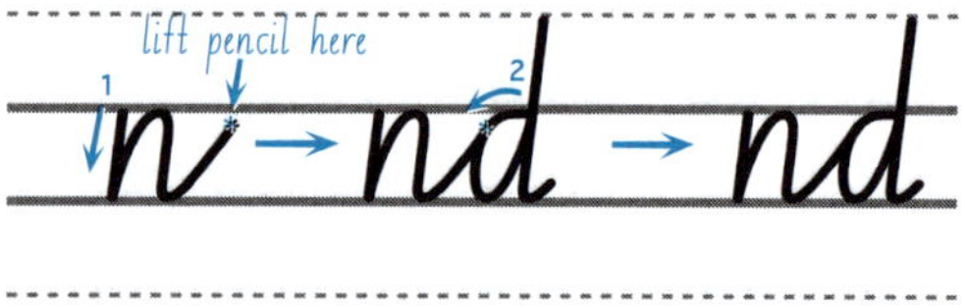

Trace

nd ca mo ag ec

Trace then copy.

ca ua ma cc tc ic id

ad nd dd ig dg ng do

mo co aq la uc ua ed

ag lo to no eq ia ha

Trace then copy.

ac ec eg ug nq ud ca

ca ua ma cc tc ic id

mo co aq la uc ua ed

ag lo to no eq ia ha

ad nd dd ig dg ng do

ac ec eg ug nq ud ca

Drop-in joins to new f with a tail

Drop in f. Write the letter f with a tail now. Make sure the exit flick meets the f at the point where the bar of the f crosses at the top solid line.

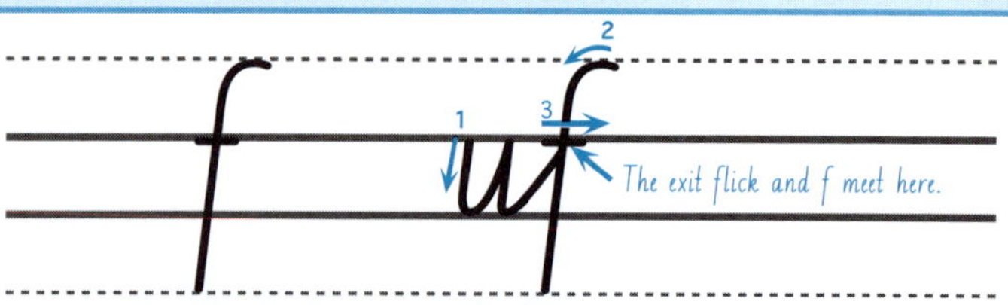

Trace

af uf nf ef if

Trace then copy.

f f f f f f f

af uf ef if lf ef nf

mf df af uf ef if lf

if nf mf df af uf ef

Horizontal joins

Letters that finish at the top solid line (o r v w x) join horizontally to the next letter.

om oy ow

Trace

om oy ow oi on

Trace then copy.

om oy oi on or ou op

ow ox oz ov om oy oi

on or ou op ow ox oz

ov om oy oi on or ou

Horizontal joins

Letters that finish at the top solid line (o r v w x) join horizontally to the next letter.

rm ry rp

Trace

rm ry rp rr ru

Trace then copy.

ri rm rn ry rv rw ru

rr rp ri rm rn ry rv

rw ru rr rp ri rm rn

ry rv rw ru rr rp ri

Letters that finish at the top solid line (o r v w x) join horizontally to the next letter.

vu wi wr

Trace

vu wi wr vy wn

Trace then copy.

vi vu vy wi wn wr vi

vu vy wi wn wr vi vu

vy wi wn wr vi vu vy

wi wn wr vi vu vy wi

Horizontal joins

Letters that finish at the top solid line (o r v w x) join horizontally to the next letter.

wu xi xy

Trace

wu xi xy wm xp

Trace then copy.

wu wm xi xp xu xy wu

wm xi xp xu xy wu wm

xi xp xu xy wu wm xi

xp xu xy wu wm xi xp

Horizontal joins to anticlockwise letters c a d o q g

To make a horizontal join to an anticlockwise letter (c a d o q g) go across to the letter's start and then retrace backwards.

od rc wa

Trace

od rc wa vo rg

Trace then copy.

oa oc og oo od ra rc

rd rg ro va vo wa wo

xa xc xo xq oa oc og

od ra rc rd rg ro va

Horizontal joins to anticlockwise letters c a d o q g

Trace then copy.

vo wa wo xa xc xo xq

oa oc og od oo ra rc

rd rg ro va vo wa wo

xa xc xo xq oa oc og

od oo ra rc rd rg ro

va vo wa wo xa xc xo

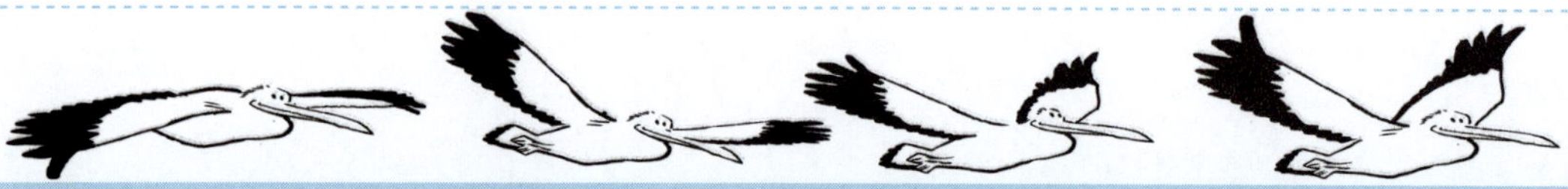

Horizontal joins from f

Join f to i, r or u with a straight horizontal line. When you join f to l, go up and then retrace down. You also have to retrace when you join from f to o or a because they are anticlockwise letters. For ff, drop in the second f without a join. Then draw the crossbar straight across both letters. Note that f does not join to the letter e.

fr fl fa ff

Trace

fr fl fa ff fo

Trace then copy.

fi fr fa fo fu fl ff

fi fr fa fo fu fl ff

fi fr fa fo fu fl ff

fi fr fa fo fu fl ff

Horizontal joins to tall letters

When you make a horizontal join to a tall letter you need to go up and then carefully retrace down.

ob rk wk

Trace

ob rk wk xt of

Trace then copy.

ob ot oh ol of rl rk

rt rb wk wh wt xt

ob ot oh ol of rl rk

rt rb wk wh wt xt

b g j p s y—letters that do not join to the next letter

Letters that finish in an anticlockwise direction (pointing backwards) don't join to the letter that comes after them. For now, also do not join to the letter s to any other letter.

b g j p s y

Trace then copy.

bat bet bin boy bump brim blip

gab get girl got gum grit grim

jam jet jump jot jest jut just

pat pet pit pot pun plop pry

sat set sit sold sum slip sprig

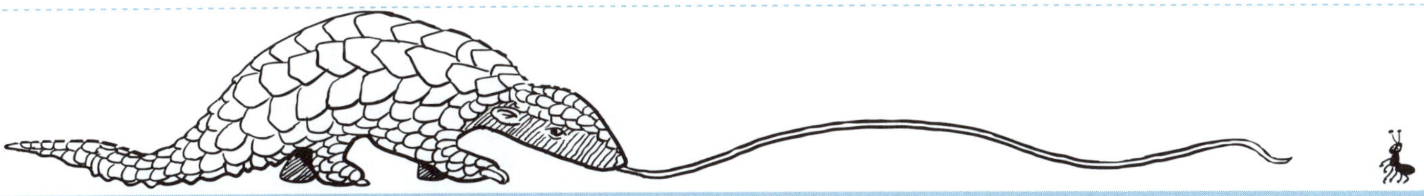

f o r v w x—letters that do not join to e

The letter e doesn't join after f o r v w x. Note also that you don't need to do entry flicks at the beginning of words.

fe oe re ve we xe

Trace then copy.

fell felt fend toe foe rent

ream realm real revere

vet vex vent veal vest rest

wet well went west welt

axe oxen boxes fixed taxes

Practising words: short letters to short letters

The words on the following pages will help you to practise all the joins you need for cursive handwriting.

Trace then copy.

antennae program aisle

ailment aimless waist aisle

diagram program exam scam

antibiotic antihistamine

argument argumentative

PARENT TIP: The following pages provide opportunities to practise and consolidate cursive writing. They also introduce your child to a wide range of vocabulary. Discuss word meanings as well as aspects of handwriting. Read the words with your child. Examine spelling patterns and discuss the different sounds made by spelling patterns such as *ae* and *ai*.

Practising words: short letters to short letters

Trace then copy.

automobile automatic aunt

celebrate celebration

cinquain circle civilian

criticism criticise critical

cute acute cube ridiculous

peekaboo weird dozen

PARENT TIP: Remind your child that the focus diagonal joins on this page join letters smoothly from exits to entry flicks. Check that letters are evenly spaced and that the slope of the letters is consistent.

Find a word from either page 42 or 43 that matches the picture. Write it on the line.

Remember how to join from *e*.

em er

Trace then copy.

weird toeing leisure weight

gremlin tremble mayhem empty

venom juvenile urgent dozen

itchier jazzier scarier verb

PARENT TIP: Remind your child to check their posture, page position and pencil grip so that their writing can be smooth and unstrained. Point out the *ei* spelling in *weird*, *weight* and *leisure*. Discuss adjectives that compare: *itchier*, *jazzier*, *scarier*, *happiest*, *jerkiest*. The word answer is *automobile*.

Practising words: short letters to short letters

Trace then copy.

amateur museum sleuth feud

whatever whomever whenever

reward unscrew strewn beware

cavities apologies loneliest

immigrant immigrate immense

microbe microscope mincingly

PARENT TIP: Ask your child to point out some of the unusual spelling patterns on the page, such as *eu*. Discuss how the *y* changes to *i* when *lonely* becomes *loneliest* and in plurals such as *cavities* and *apologies*.

Find a word from either page 44 or 45 that matches the picture. Write it on the line.

Remember how to do diagonal joins.

ir me mn

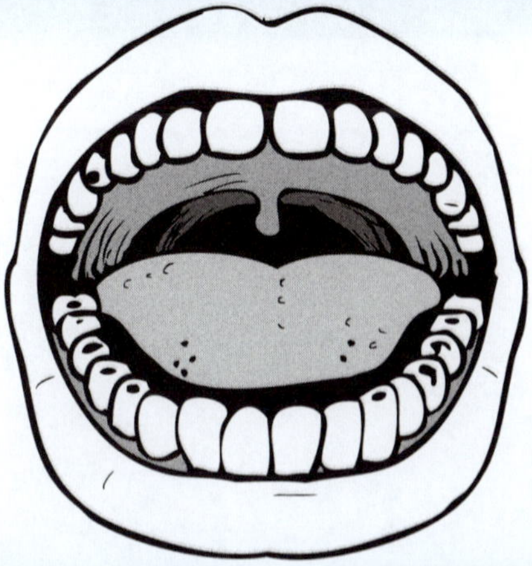

Trace then copy.

inspire awesome museum

swirl squirt squirm shirk

awesome gruesome fearsome

solemn gymnast mnemonic

PARENT TIP: Talk about the words and their meanings. Encourage your child to use the words in sentences. Challenge your child to add a number of new words to conversations every day and to use new words such as *awesome*, *gruesome* and *fearsome* in their writing. The word answer is *cavities*.

Practising words: short letters to short letters

Trace then copy.

amnesia lasagne new hygiene

immunise sanitise volcanic

stunning unnerving annoying

snuggle numb peanut nudge

guest guess guessing guest

impossible adventure guess

PARENT TIP: Watch the gap between the letters. Talk about the spelling pattern *ue* in *guest*, *guess* and *guessing*. Use an internet word search to find other words with the *ue* spelling: *queue*, *barbecue*, *residue*. More *ue* words are included on the next page. Discuss the different sounds made by *ue*.

Find a word from either page 46 or 47 that matches the picture. Write it on the line.

Watch that your letter spaces are even.

um ur ue

Trace then copy.

rescue meringue fatigue

vacuum volume triumph rumour

future adventure treasure

survive honour courtesy furry

PARENT TIP: Point out the *our* pattern in *rumour*, *honour* and *courtesy*. Use an internet search to find other words with this pattern. Make rhyming words. The *uu* in *vacuum* is a rare spelling pattern. It is also in *continuum* and *residuum*. The word answer is *treasure*.

Practising words: short letters to long letters

Trace then copy.

majestic major majority ajar

apology apiarist appetite ape

cyberspace literacy numeracy

eyesight journey kidneys

creep creepier creepiest

occupy occupant interrupt

PARENT TIP: Your child has to think about spelling as they write so they can make allowances in the lengths of the exit flicks; otherwise the letters won't touch smoothly.

Choose one word from either page 48 or 49 and draw a picture to match. Write the word on the line.

Be careful when you join these letters.

ep ej mp

Trace then copy.

creepily crept creepily crept

eject reject dejected rejoice

buy buyout buyer buying

impair umpire swampy simplest

PARENT TIP: Remind your child that the letters *b*, *g*, *j*, *p*, *s* and *y* do not join to the next letter because they end with an anticlockwise movement. Make word families for words such as *creep*: *creeps*, *creepiest*, *creeper*, *creepier*. Note how the spelling changes. Make a word family for *buy*. Discuss how the spelling changes for the past tense: *bought*.

Practising words: short letters to long letters

Trace then copy.

myth mysterious mythical

autonomy alchemy enemy

homonym antonym synonym

nylon vinyl peony acronym

currency cyclist recycle

illness myth bulbous

PARENT TIP: The *y*, *s* and *p* in many of these words are anticlockwise letters that do not join to the letter after them.

Practising words: tall letters to tall letters

Choose one word from either page 50 or 51 and draw a picture to match. Write the word on the line.

Remember how to join to a tall letter.
Go up and then retrace down.

lt lk lb

Trace then copy.

quilt guilt penalty moult

folklore folktale townsfolk

folksong walkway walkout

bulb bulbous elbow mulberry

PARENT TIP: Watch how your child retraces letters l, t, k and b after joining them to other letters in the focus pairs on this page. Are the retracing movements neat and careful? Discuss the compound words on the page. Think of others to add to the word families.

Practising words: tall letters to tall letters

Trace then copy.

thousand fourth twentieth

warthog weather wealth wreath

jittery flattery fluttery motto

spluttery unflattering

dependable reckless wrinkly

health stealth wealth

PARENT TIP: Check that the retracing of the head and body letters after the diagonal joins are neat and that the letters are evenly spaced. Point out the *-th* ending on the number words. These are ordinal numbers: *first*, *second*, *third*, *fourth*, *fifth*, *sixth*, and so on. Talk to your child about occasions when people might use ordinal numbers.

Practising words: short letters to tall letters

Find a word from either page 52 or 53 that matches the picture. Write it on the line.

Remember how to join to a tall letter. You go up and then retrace down.

at ab al

Trace then copy.

stealth ideal ethical wealth

breathe empathy create attend

likeable dependable capable

address adorable add addition

PARENT TIP: There are many words on this page with the spelling pattern *ea*. Read the words and help your child hear the different sounds. Make a list of words with the suffix *-able* and talk about the meaning that *-able* brings to them. Discuss the word *empathy* and its meaning. The word answer is *warthog*.

Practising words: short letters to tall letters

Trace then copy.

akimbo awaken sneaking croaks

submarine submerge subtract

ukulele sukiyaki yukky fluke

ghoul rule would should mould

out outsmart outswim outwait

rumble lifeboat submerge

PARENT TIP: Watch how your child makes a diagonal join from a short letter to a tall letter on this page. Is it smooth and fluent? Is the retracing smooth and careful? Does your child leave too much space between *s* and other letters? It takes practice to judge how much space *s* needs because it starts with an anticlockwise movement.

Find a word from either page 54 or 55 that matches the picture. Write it on the line.

Remember how to join to a tall letter. You go up and then retrace down.

mb ek et

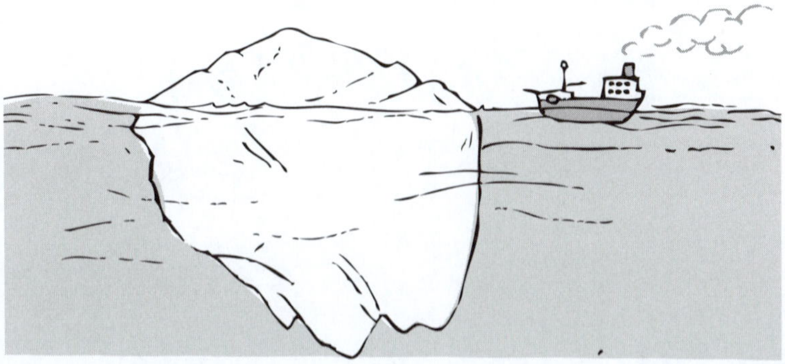

Trace then copy.

sleek weekly meekly trekking

iceberg lifeboat pebbles debris

fidget widget greet petition

bearlike wartlike bike spike

PARENT TIP: There's a silent *b* in *crumb* and a silent *s* in *debris*. Talk about the suffix -*like* in *bearlike* and *wartlike*. Think of other compound words with -*like* at the end and what they mean: *childlike*, *snakelike*, *crablike*. The word answer is *iceberg*.

Practising words: short letters to tall letters

Trace then copy.

gloomily drowsily crankily

withheld withdrew biscuit suit

dribble quibble invincible

ache schedule chemist choice

chuckle fiddlesticks decide

hearty loathe clothe hyphen

PARENT TIP: Words ending in -ly are adverbs. They add meaning to verbs to tell how. Talk about the sounds made by ch in words on this page.

Practising words: tall letters to short letters

Choose one word from either page 56 or 57 and draw a picture to match. Write the word on the line.

de dr he

Trace then copy.

decide decide decide

dinosaur disease disagree

dread drizzle draught dragon

deduce dustiest dubious duty

PARENT TIP: Read the words with your child and discuss their meanings. Use the words in sentences for your child. Help your child learn to spell the words.

Practising words: tall letters to short letters

Trace then copy.

munching sloshing whistling

huggable humour thundery

embarked unlikely wicked

freakiest muckiest skulkiest

knuckles knobbly knees know

sickroom slime scull

PARENT TIP: Point out the silent *k* in words on this page and the silent *t* in *whistling*. The *y* changes to an *i* in adjectives such as *freakiest*. Watch how your child joins the *f* to the *r* in *freakiest*.

Choose one word from either page 58 or 59 and draw a picture to match. Write the word on the line.

kr lm

Trace then copy.

breakup backup lockup skull

agile allergic electric leave

slime finalist holiday replica

calm helmet palm film almond

PARENT TIP: Talk about the compound words on this page and the silent *l* in *calm*, *palm* and *almond*. Watch how your child manages the join from *l* to *e*. Is it smooth?

Practising words: tall letters to short letters

Trace then copy.

clumsy clumsy glumly flurry

mystery athlete affectionate

Arctic Atlantic Antarctica

trickier trickiest trickster

nature nocturnal turmoil tussled

tricky trickier trickster

PARENT TIP: Ask your child to identify the proper nouns on the page. Use an atlas to find other proper-noun placenames that begin with upper-case *A*. Discuss the meanings of *trickster* and *nocturnal*.

Practising words: tall letters to long letters

Find a word from either page 60 or 61 that matches the picture. Write it on the line.

dy ky

Trace then copy.

remedy comedy cloudy

why squelchy physical rhythm

backyard junkyard skydiver

finicky skylight skywards pesky

PARENT TIP: Ask your child to identify the compound words on this page. Point out the sound made by *ph* in *physical*, the silent *h* after the *r* in *rhythm* and the soft *j* sound made by *g* in *tragedy*. The word answer is *nocturnal*.

Practising words: tall letters to long letters

Trace then copy.

terribly shoddily sly

celebrity minority humidity

charity style platypus

trudged edge judge porridge

hedgehog dodge dislodge

trudged edge judge porridge

PARENT TIP: Point out the sound made by *dg* in *trudged*, *edge*, *judge*, *porridge*, *hedgehog*, *dodge* and *dislodge*. Add rhyming words to create word lists. Use an internet search to find synonyms for *trudged*.

Practising words: diagonal joins from *q* and *z*

Find a word from either page 62 or 63 that matches the picture. Write it on the line.

qu zy

Trace then copy.

quirky quirkily quoits

aquatic queasy squash

consequence plaque squalor

zilch zest puzzle lazy

PARENT TIP: Check that your child is joining *q* and *z* correctly to the letters that follow them. Remind your child that *z* has a wave on the main line. Ask your child what they think of their own writing or any difficulties they are having. The word answer is *squash*.

Practising words: joining to *f*

Trace then copy.

whiff skiff sift gifts unify

waft draft baffle affix

ruffle duffle buffer guffaw

befall woeful useful refuel

falsify terrify liquify

PARENT TIP: Check how your child joins *f* and especially how your child writes *ff*. Remind them that *f* does not join to *e* in words such as *buffer*. One crossbar goes across two letters in *ft* and *ff*.

Practising words: horizontal joins

Choose one word from either page 64 or 65 and draw a picture to match. Write the word on the line.

or ow om

Trace then copy.

breakdown townhouse coward

humorous gorgeous perilous

minion action fraction potion

boredom common woman phantom

PARENT TIP: Remind your child to keep their letters evenly spaced and of a consistent slope. Read the words with your child and discuss meanings. Challenge your child to use some of the words in sentences.

Practising words: horizontal joins

Trace then copy.

Remember that the letter *o* joins horizontally. To join *o* to a tall letter remember to go up and then carefully retrace down.

opposite lollipop jeopardy

voyage loyal joyfully boycott

bulldoze froze doze mozzarella

pollution chocolate collection

obliging problem lobster

PARENT TIP: Ask your child to read the words to you and then to use each word in a sentence. Explain the meanings of any unfamiliar words or help your child use a dictionary to find the words.

Find a word from either page 66 or 67 that matches the picture. Write it on the line.

Remember that *o*, *r*, *w* and *x* join horizontally to tall letters. Go up then retrace down.

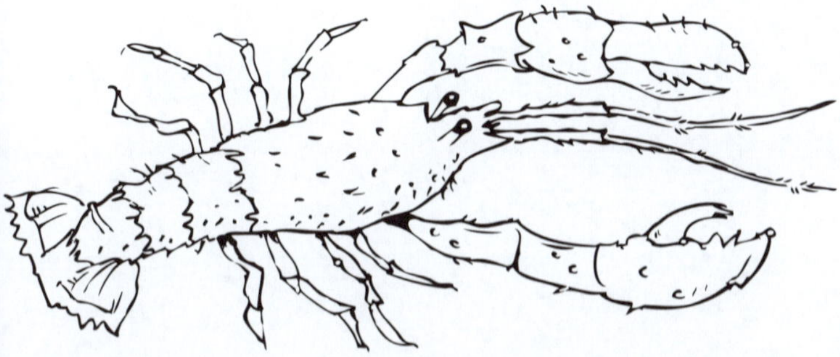

Trace then copy.

cohort coherent aloha

barley clearly unfurl yearly

market work embark murky

certificate participate carport

PARENT TIP: Read the words. Discuss the silent *t* in *depot*. Notice if your child is having difficulty with any particular joins or letters. Is their fluency impeded on some letters or joins more than others? Check the position of the writing page and your child's wrist and hand. Are there physical adjustments that might help your child manage their writing more easily? The word answer is *lobster*.

Practising words: horizontal joins

Trace then copy.

suburb carbon turban blurb

hawk squawk gawking hawklike

owlets yowled howled bowled

growth overgrowth blurb

foxlike boxlike waxlike

PARENT TIP: Read the words with your child. Help them pronounce the words. Is your child using small dips for the horizontal joins at *ow* in many of these words? Is your child's posture correct to avoid neck and wrist strain? Is your child's speed at writing increasing without sacrificing legibility?

Practising words: horizontal joins to drop-in letters

Find a word from either page 68 or 69 that matches the picture. Write it on the line.

Remember that when joining horizontally to anticlockwise letters *a*, *c*, *o*, *g* and *d* you go across and then retrace anticlockwise.

Trace then copy.

ventriloquist ventriloquism

ocelot docile doctor lockdown

bamboozle outdoors zookeeper

epilogue dialogue prologue

PARENT TIP: When making a horizontal join to an anticlockwise letter; for example, from *o* to *a*, *c*, *g*, *o* or *q* check that your child does a smooth horizontal join and then retraces neatly across the top of the anticlockwise letter. Discuss meanings for words in the word families *ventriloquy*, *ventriloquist*, *ventriloquism* and *epilogue*, *dialogue*, *prologue* and *eulogy*. The word answer is *ventriloquist*.

Practising words: diagonal join to *o* from *t*, *h* or *l*

Trace then copy.

risotto tomato tomatoes

pesto pronto stomach

cacophony honesty symphony

hullabaloo garrulous logical

flood allowance global

PARENT TIP: Remind your child that *o* is a drop-in letter so they'll need to make the exit flick on the previous letter a little higher so it almost reaches the top solid line to allow the *o* to be dropped in.

Practising words: joining from *f*

Choose one word from either page 70 or 71 and draw a picture to match. Write the word on the line.

Remember that *f* joins horizontally from its crossbar. To join to *a* and *o* you go across and then retrace anticlockwise.

Trace then copy.

farfetched effective confess

difficult refill dignified

inform information informed

wasteful forceful faithful

PARENT TIP: Point out the suffix -*ful*. Discuss the meaning it adds to words. Check that the joins from the *f* are neat and that the retracing to join *f* to *o* and *a* is also neat.

Trace then copy.

frequent alfresco friendly

flute flutist florist flavour

deft weft left graft shaft

baffled muffle waffle scuffle

buffeted effect sniffles

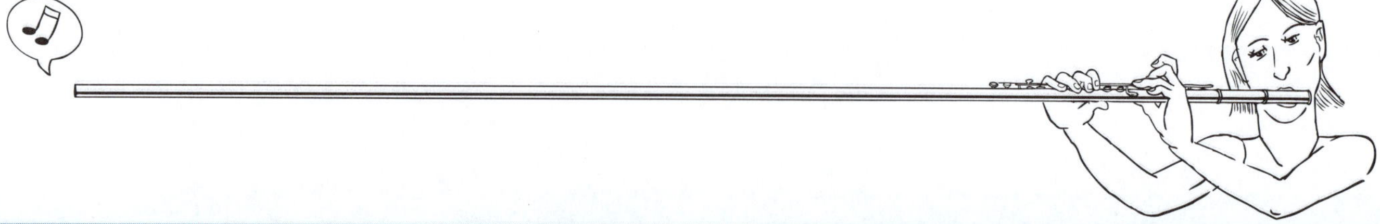

PARENT TIP: Have your child read the words aloud. Ask if they know the meaning of all the words. Use a dictionary to clarify any meanings. Use the words in conversations. Check how your child manages the diagonal join from f to l. Ask your child to reflect on their cursive writing and to honestly state which areas could improve and which areas they are pleased with.

Writing cursive sentences

Trace then copy.

Agile Anne ached from her

adventure around Antarctica.

Baffled bears on bikes

ate barley in the backyard.

Charlie calmly celebrated

her certificate with chocolate.

PARENT TIP: These sentences use the vocabulary words already presented in the book. Help your child create some alliterative sentences of their own.

Trace then copy.

The dragon dribbled on the

doctor so dialogue was

dreadfully difficult.

Erin's eyesight was not

effective in

her exam.

Trace then copy.

The film was farfetched so

Fred was frequently fidgety.

Gail was gleefully glamping

in the gorge.

Kelvin knows

his knees are knobbly.

Trace then copy.

'Honestly,' said Hetty. 'That

hedgehog is not huggable.'

The loneliest lobster left

the lifeboat to look for love.

Penny was puzzled

by the prologue.

Trace then copy.

The owlets outwaited the ocelot

in the overgrowth.

Paul ate peanuts and

porridge at the park.

Meringue and mozzarella

make the muckiest meal.

Trace then copy.

Reggie is reckless

and rejects rules.

The solemn sleuth

had the sniffles on Saturday.

The townsfolk tussled over

thousands of tomatoes.

Trace then copy.

The woeful warthog had a

wartlike welt at its waist.

The woman was whistling at

work on Wednesday.

Zara the zookeeper was zealous

at zebra duties.

Revision: rhyme

Trace then write a rhyming word underneath.

hike farm stumpy sleep

stumble rose thread snuffle

ledge gape foursome raffle

dye buckle aloud bumpy

slept chokes suit theft

lodge raft bread rude

The words on these pages all rhyme with words used on the practising words pages 41–72. If you can't think of a rhyming word yourself, check those pages. Remember that rhyme is about the sounds in words so rhyming words don't always have the same spelling patterns (*file*, *aisle*).

Trace then write a rhyming word underneath.

action those blurry shifts

fool stamping plate sheet

less jest quilt fork

wealth pelmet broad growled

siphon snazzier fudge peas

toe hazy grieve foil

Revision: rhyme

Trace then copy.

weakly grotto old crunching

perky chew pith history

grudge thumb pylon shout

charm shark solution ruffle

gram guzzle easy nibble

lotion lurk humour wood

Trace then write a rhyming word underneath.

lift tiff dull sheik

dry peaking column worm

running dial urban herb

haste stealth gate sky

plucky pest verify hewn

peeking shy dramatise

Revision: word families

Add words to the columns to make word families. Use your best cursive handwriting.

crumble	crumbling	crumbled
cycle		
decided		
dozes		
examined		
flooding		
impossibility		
informative		
puzzling		
trickiest		
withdrawing		
wrinkled		

PARENT TIP: Help your child write different kinds of words such as verbs in different tenses (*crumbling*, *crumbled*, *crumbles*); adjectives (*crumbly* biscuit, *crumbling* biscuit); nouns (apple *crumble*); and adverbs (*decidedly*). Check spellings with your child.

addition		
allowance		
annoying		
apologise		
boredom		
squashy		
squawked		
survival		
swirl		
tempted		
triumphant		
wealthiest		

Revision: labels

Here are some labels from a museum exhibition. Fill in the gaps so there's a label in each column.

Upper-case	Cursive
GARRIGARANG	
	Sea Country
	Salt Water People
	shell midden
COMMUNITY	
	ghost net
SHELL STRINGING	
BARK PAINTING	
	bark canoe
SEASONAL CALENDAR	
	totem
PLANT FIBRES	
ANIMAL FUR	

PARENT TIP: On this page there are no guidelines. Check that your child is writing letters of consistent size and slope, and that letters are level across an imaginary bottom line.

List ten things you can see in your bedroom. Practise upper-case and lower-case printing and cursive.

Upper-case	Print	Cursive
WARDBROBE	wardrobe	wardrobe

Extra advanced joins: horizontal and diagonal joins to *s*

Join *s* horizontally after letters which end on the top solid line (*r*, *o*, *v*, *w*, *x* and *f*). The horizontal join goes over the top of *s* and then retraces.

fs rs os

Trace then copy.

rs vs ws xs fs rs xs

gears rivers person worst

hoofs almost those drowsy

news gnaws jaws flaxseed

offside offstage yours meows

PARENT TIP: This join is mostly taught in Year 4. We're showing your child here because joining *s* makes handwriting faster. If you find this join makes your child's cursive writing illegible, then tell your child to leave it until a later time.

Join s diagonally after letters that end at the main line (a, c, d, e, h, i, k, l, m, n, t, u, z). The diagonal join goes to the top and a little way over the start of s. Notice the top of the s is a little shorter than usual.

as es ts

Trace then copy.

as cs ds es hs is ks

ls ms ns ts us zs ts

asleep critics gadgets crowds

resource distress youths chorus

wisdom zooms answer usable

PARENT TIP: The shape of s changes a little for a diagonal join. Make sure your child spaces letters evenly and that their writing remains fluid and legible.

Extra advanced joins: horizontal joins to *e*

To join *e* horizontally after letters which end on the top solid line (*r*, *o*, *v*, *w*, *x*) you need to exit and then dip down far enough to start the loop of the *e*.

oe re we ve xe

Trace then copy.

re oe ve we xe re oe

entirely nature stream brave

canoed poem joey venom

weather weak lovely hives

fixes coaxed exercise exert

PARENT TIP: We're showing your child how to do this join because joining *e* horizontally can make handwriting faster. If you find this join makes your child's cursive writing illegible, then tell your child to leave it until a later time.

Trace then copy.

Sven canoed downstream

entirely enjoying nature.

Olive loves exercise.

She also writes lovely poems.

Olive and Sven coaxed a

weak joey away from hives.

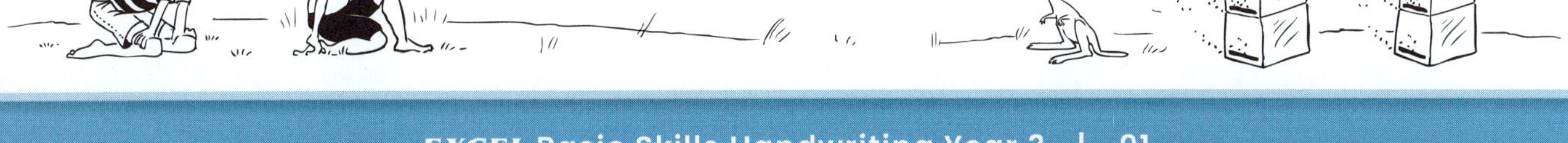

Self-assessment

Before you start work on this page you need to get organised so you can time yourself writing.

Time yourself as you copy each pangram using Foundation printing. Record your time.

The quick brown fox jumps over the lazy dog.

Time:

We saw five boxing zombies quickly run to jump the ditch.

Time:

Time yourself as you copy each pangram using cursive writing. Record your time.

The quick brown fox jumps over the lazy dog.

Time:

We saw five boxing zombies quickly run to jump the ditch.

Time:

Answer the questions about the handwriting you did on the previous page.

Circle your answers.

Which was faster?	printing	cursive
Which is easier to read?	printing	cursive
Which is easier for you to write?	printing	cursive
Which do you prefer to use?	printing	cursive

Rate your cursive writing (1 = needs a lot of improvement; 5 = excellent)

Is the writing easy to read?	1	2	3	4	5
Are my letters evenly spaced? Circle any letter pairs not evenly spaced.	1	2	3	4	5
Is the slope consistent? Circle any letters not consistently sloped.	1	2	3	4	5
Have I joined *q* neatly? Circle *q*.	1	2	3	4	5
Is my retracing neat?	1	2	3	4	5
Are diagonal joins perfect? Circle any letter joins needing improvement.	1	2	3	4	5
Are my drop-in joins evenly spaced and connected? Circle any drop-in joins needing improvement.	1	2	3	4	5
Are all horizontal joins perfect? Circle any horizontal joins needing improvement.	1	2	3	4	5
Does *f* have a neat new tail? Circle *f*.	1	2	3	4	5

Is my grip on the pencil relaxed and my pencil pressure comfortable?	never	sometimes	always
Do I have any neck, arm or wrist strain when writing for long periods of time?	never	sometimes	always

In what three ways could I improve my writing? Comment.

Overall I think my cursive writing is

NSW Foundation Style Cursive

Exits and entries

a b c d e f g h i j k l m

n o p q r s t u v w x y z

Diagonal joins from letters with exits near the main line

ai um er my de uk qu zi

Drop-in joins to *a c d g o q f*

ca uc nd eg mo nq nf

Horizontal joins from *o r v w x f*

oi rm vy wu xy fr

Letters that don't join to the next letter: *b g j p s y*

bat grim just pry sum yet

Letters that don't join to e: *o r v w x f*

foe rent vet web axe fell

Double *f* and joined *ft*

scuffle effect raft left fifty

Advanced horizontal and diagonal joins to *s*

os rs ws fs as es is ls ns ts

Advanced horizontal joins to *e*

jewel pixels brave shoes nature

Numerals

0 1 2 3 4 5 6 7 8 9

Punctuation

. , ? ! “ ”

‘ ’

: ; –

Posture, paper tilt and pencil/pen grip

Posture

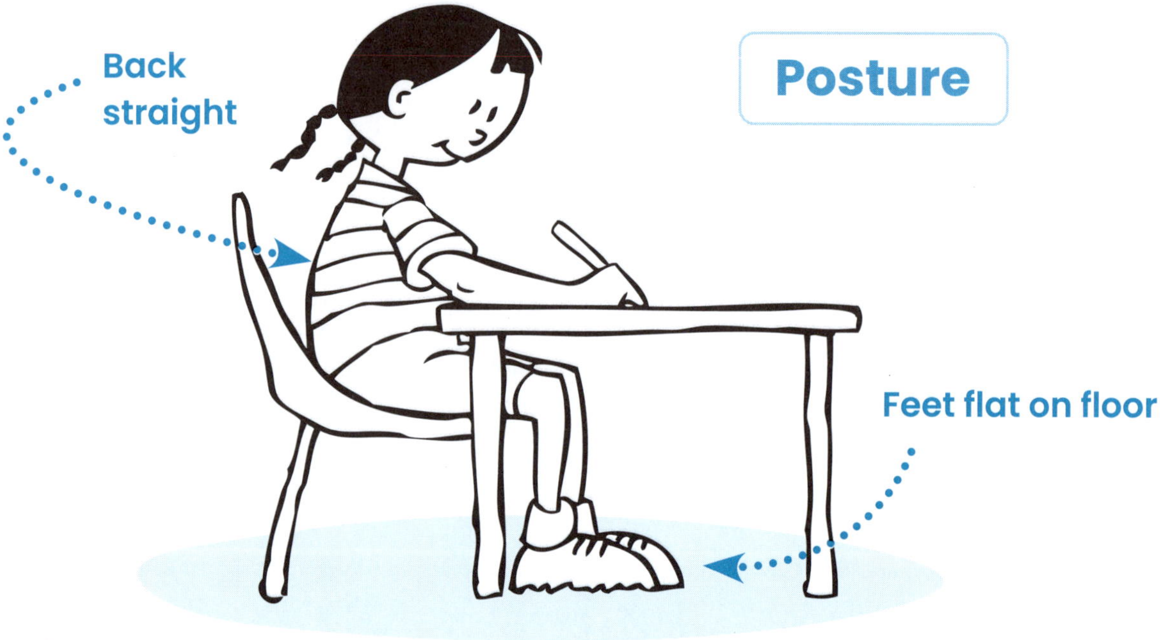

Paper tilt

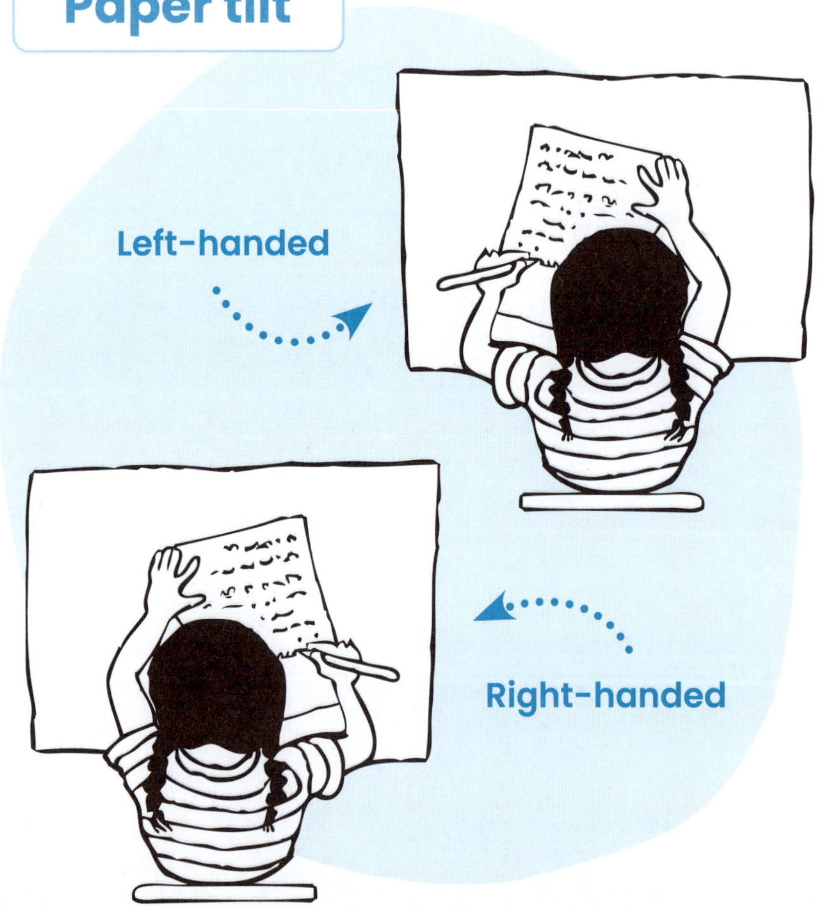

Pencil/Pen grip

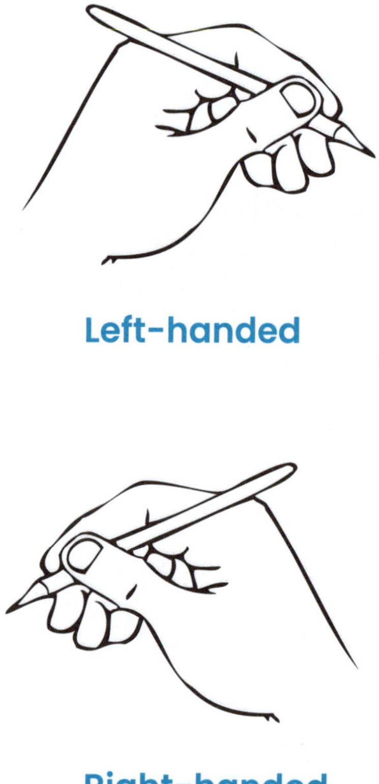